I See You Mocha Mocha

Alyshia Bradley

I See You Mocha Mocha

By Alyshia Bradley

Copyright 2021 by Alyshia Bradley

All Rights Reserved

To contact the author:
Email: alyshia.bradley@yahoo.com
Facebook: Honestly, Mocha Goddess
Artist's Instagram: honestly_mochagoddess

Photo Credits:
Gershawn Mason
Anthony Montgomery

I See You Mocha Mocha

4 year olds cannot tiptoe.
So that's only what I thought I was doing, making my way slowly,
loudly tehehe
Down the hall to her
The woman with my face
Peeking around the corner
At the woman with my smile
With my master plan to scare her
And oh trust me I had a back up for her goooooOooood if my rawr should fail!
Hmph and teheheheeee too
I have her face
I look like she do.
She is working, papers, calculator, checkbook, ha!
Good.
Now crawl, she can't see you past the chairs.
She can't feel the movement in the floor now that you're 2 feet away from her and your "lizard"
isn't too stealthy.
You've got her.
…..RA-
"What are you doing little girl ? "
Say nothing! Don't speak!
I see you Mocha Mocha
Giggles ensue
You laugh like me
I laugh like you
Chin on table
Mommy mommy would you still love me if I looked like
this??
I twisted my face into something horrible!
Of course I will silly, I'm your mommy.
Beam
Love bursting at the seams
I asked the same thing a lot as a teen
without words
but the intent was the same
Sometimes I think I actually scared her
My attitude double dared her
My troubles I kept unaware to her
And that cost.
I am her child.
I have her face.

*Mommy Mommy would you still love me if I looked like
this?*
To me my face had changed.
Damaged from loss and rain.
*In my 20s I made it even worse by answering to anything
other than my name.*
From her I demanded space.
*I couldn't even look in the mirror most days knowing she
would be there.*
I had not forgotten my own plan
Or the failure
Just to wait for her reply
And then at age 28 I died.
*Mommy mommy would you still love me if I looked like
this?*
I am my mother's child.
And so I have her pain too
That is also how I'm able to keep smiling like she do
Laughing like she do
Fighting like she do
Loving like she do
We have the same fire
We do.
And say
Mommy mommy would you still love me if I looked like this ?
And this time,
This time and from now on
I will stay
To hear you say
"Of course I will silly, I'm your mommy."
Beam.
Love bursting at the seams.

Table of Contents

Trigger Warning: May reference subject matters that readers will find upsetting

As I lay me down to sleep, I pray this art my soul to keep. And as I live so human this way,

I pray The Lord these laments He takes.

A lament: (Biblically speaking) a cry to God for Him to intervene

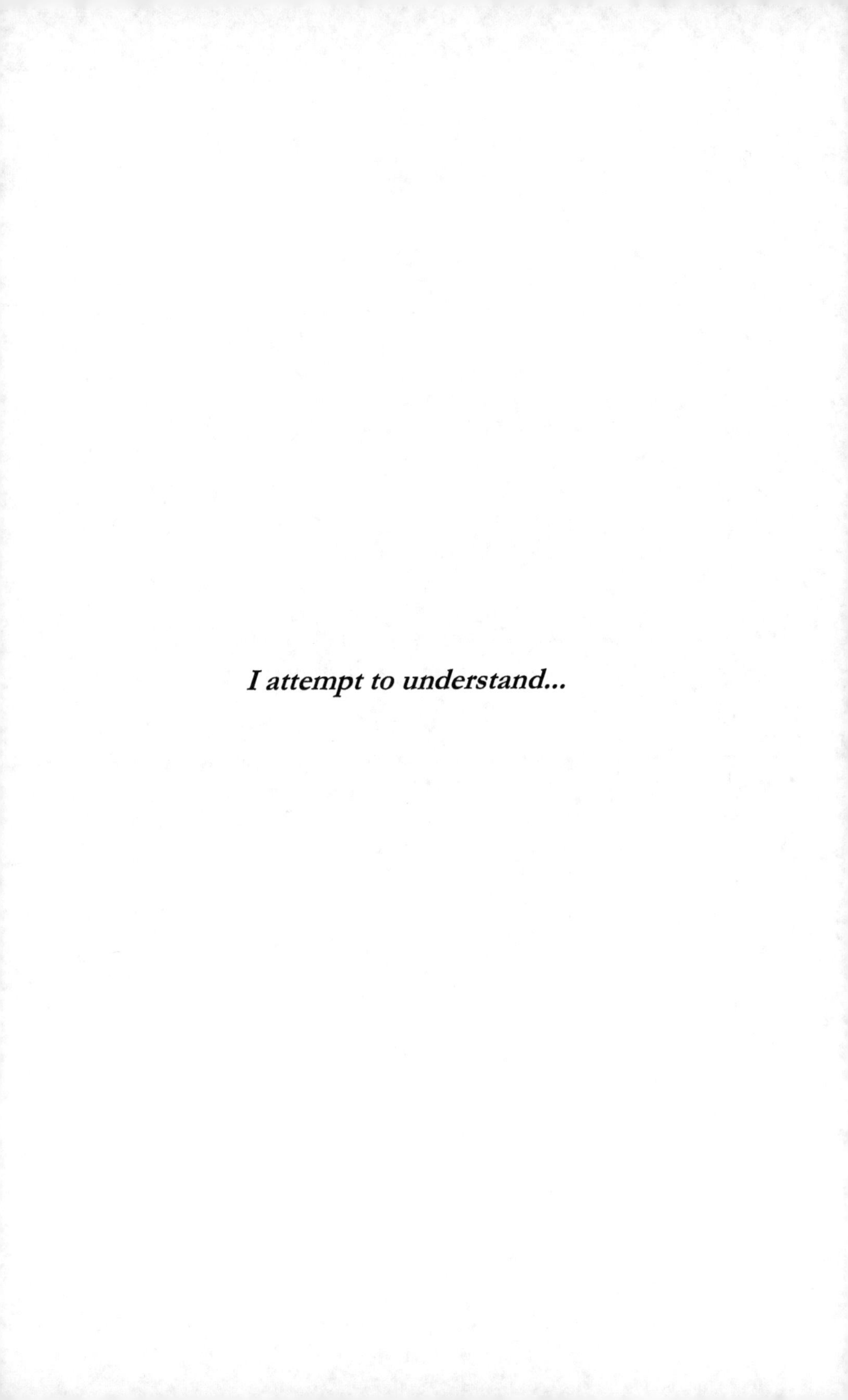

I attempt to understand...

Walk First

We both want to know If the other

Can handle holding a cup of

tea,

While eyes watch God.

Parallel.

Closest proximity.

Him

Me Tea

A larger portion for our feelings of loneliness. Because we both know,

We do not belong here.

But for now,

In closest proximity as possible, Watching God.

We walk.

His firm hands in constant caress. Mine, fingers laced,

In constant prayer,.

His eyes tearful

Fearful with joy at such love. And mine the same.

We walk.

Let You In

You coax forward a woman as I reach. Sing softly as I sleep.

I've mixed paint the color of your skin exactly. You sigh as well as me,

And every time you are around Love, a calm threat like a dam. I submissive in your hands, And bright in your eyes.

Me sweet on your lips,

And you on my heart in my prayers. I swear.

I've seen you dance in storms, And quiet my heart enough To let you in.

Soft and Vibrant

And He said:

You look very soft and vibrant Bathing in the silence

Kissing your own skin with your fingertips. Your walk has a rhythm girl

Your talk stirs the feelings girl Please.

Look my way so soft and vibrant.

Fill up the silence with moans and giggles Prayers and dreams

And thoughts of me and you And us.

Bathe me in your glory.

Please.

I need you To want me.

One Hell of a Kiss

How dare I have such a body?

So says the beauty mark on my left thigh. I can feel your lips there,

And everywhere else.

Intoxicating.

You delicious delicious man. We sigh in time.

Grazing skin with sensual whispers And hungry hands.

Meeting lip to lip Finally.

Flustered and tip toed, Blushing,

Eyes low.

It isn't fair.

How dare I have such a body? Such an arch to my back,

And tempting curves, And round breasts?

Pressed to your chest.

How dare I stir the pools in your eyes Until they are mocha brown.

And how dare you kiss me like that, And not devour me whole.

Sweat Sweet

A true intimate touch was foreign to me, Until Sweat Sweet.

With you, love from here to eternity.

I ache for every tomorrow without you, I ache for you.

Sweat Sweet,

Our love it brings me to my feet,

And when I hide between those sheets with you New life you give to me.

Sweat Sweet,

You must know what you do to me. Not submissive by nature,

But you calm the soul in me. Sweat Sweet.

Sweat Sweet.

Tell me more of your romance of my thighs, And whisper on my hips,

Because at this point, At this point,

I need you more than me. Please.

Sweat Sweet.

Strange and Lovely

Darling, do you stare more because I'm strange? Or because I'm lovely?

Dear God, I hope it is both.

That you have fallen in love with me because I am both. That way I know you love all of me.

I'm sure I was strange first to you, Awkward on what to say.

Laughing too loud and wringing my hands.

My outward response to feeling your inner power, your inner pull for me. The strange and the lovely.

You could look me in the eye and I'd probably cry at the intimacy. Lovely next because

I have a monopoly on being adorable,

And I find my collar bones and arch of my back sexy, And only partially because you said so first.

You rule my heart in a way that feels most like God's love And my father's.

Make me glad for every love I missed out on, Pushed away,

Misread,

Just for being a little too strange and a little too lovely. I cry at the intimacy.

Isn't that strange?

Isn't that lovely ?

Beggar

You stirred something in me, It isn't fair.

It simply embellished my loneliness. I ache for touch at night,

And recoil at the notion in the day. No hands are yours.

No lips are yours.

I ache to be yours.

Loneliness is dangerous.

It is all I see in other people.

Lonely hands that choke out heart beaten pleas. Lonely hands that pick and pry as they reach for me, But yours were steadfast in prayer.

I thought they were good. My hands were a pinch pot,

My eyes, weary from begging,

But you looked at me like I was Christ,

Fain to add more bread than most to my solitary hands.

A Thought of Me and You

My God, I miss you.

You were thoughtful.

Corny.

Perfect.

The kind of thought that makes heartache worth it. I miss you.

I hate that.

And I ache too,

But I deserve that.

And I need to just think of you,

To get me through all the things I had been thoughtless to. I'm a hurt person.

I've been dragging bits of me everywhere and now I swear grieving is all I think about. I don't think you thought to think of me as a dead girl.

I just think you just thought I was pretty.

And I think you just thought you were feeling me. And I think I was grateful, you were seeing me.

You called me lovely. Sat with my sadness too.

I was incomplete and lovely.

Like those famous sculptures missing their arms, Like our kisses that turned into poems,

Like my heart now that I know him. And I miss you.

And I hate that. And I ache for you, But I deserve that.

Please tell me how to swallow a thought of you. I think I need to eat healthier .

And I think,

I think I wanna die.

A thought.

A thought of me and you.

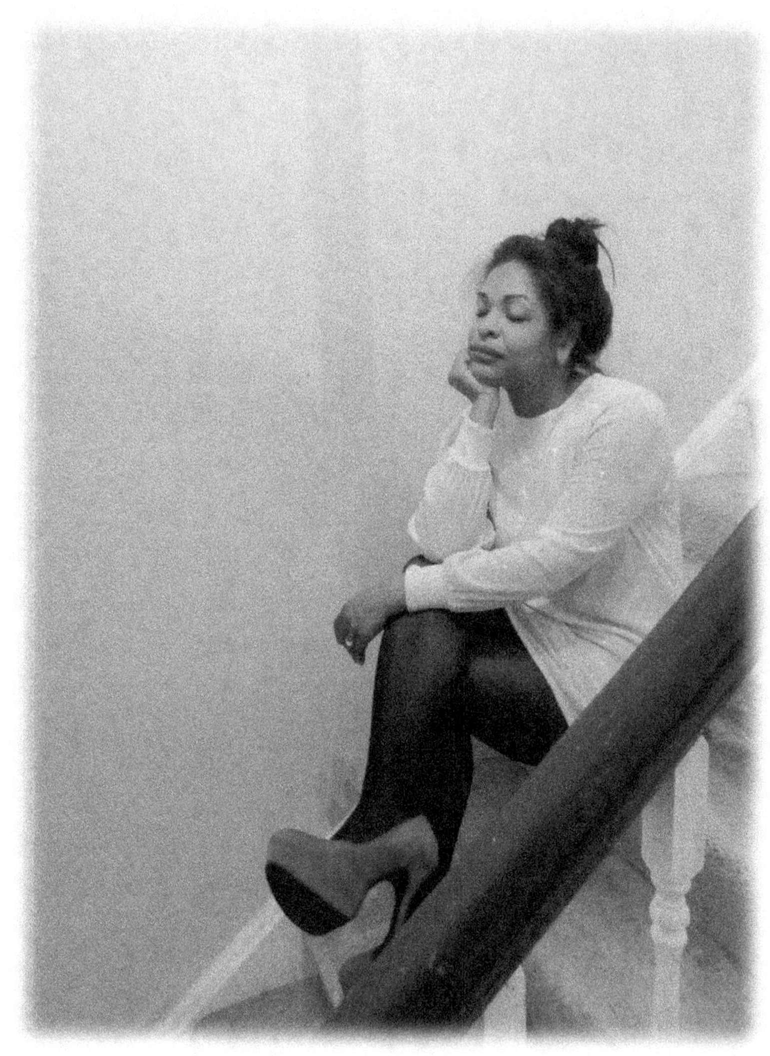

Oh, How I Try...

I Don't Feel Like Myself

I'm showing too many signs I don't know myself,

Cuz everytime I'm with you I shrink and betray myself. And as long as I'm here I'll keep ending up

By myself, Next to myself, Below myself,

But never with myself.

I miss myself.

Last seen living in between two feelings: Empowered and Ashamed.

You confuse me.

I'd forgotten my name meant protected by God, What a place to be.

It made no sense to me, And I felt by myself.

I feel by myself.

And stuck.

Next to myself.

Below myself.

But never with myself.

With you I don't feel myself.

Metaphors, Screams and Things

I think I'm becoming numb to things, Like how you don't really look at me.

And how you don't sit and think about simple things like how my hair curls, Or wedding rings.

You're not romantic just, Lonely.

But how can you be when you're holding me, remember ? Hey, I'm here!

Getting reacquainted with my oldest fear of not being enough for you. Cuz truthfully, sometimes I need to hear that shit.

That you need me.

That I'm lovely.

That you'll place no one above me. That I matter.

That you like that I'm bossy and silly and moody.

And that you notice every week how I'm impressed by the moon, Or that losing me this lifetime would be entirely too soon.

Can you look at me and cry about it? Dying to tell the world about it?

Can you look at me, eyes twinkling, like I'm the treasure you'd been looking for? Like I'm the dream you're fighting for?

Look at me!

Like you actually give a damn about my musings and grief, Like you just want to hug that shit away!

Like you miss me after a minute,

Like I'm not naive to believe in love or in you. Look at me.

Cuz your eyes are beautiful. They have me writing poetry, And hearing you in music

And forgive me all my feelings,

I hope this love is what you're seeing.

Because that's what this is, a request to be seen. Placed between metaphors, screams and things… Like love.

Love Stinks

I think smells get me the most. Today I had to throw out the lotion deodorant

body wash

and laundry detergent I smelled like when I was with you. Because now I don't sit
in your lap

Or the curve of your smile, Or my side of the bed.

No.

It is just me.

And it is weird being without you. I inhale and recall,

The smell of sweat after gigs and sex. Your favorite hoodie.

And booze on your lips that was sweet from all the kind words slurred to me.
Candles, and incense accosted my senses,

And refused to give my heart back.

I cried and breathed into the clothes returned to me, Hyper aware of the us that I
lacked.

I miss you.

I inhale and am reminded of a time when you were mine.

I remember your body wash lotion

deodorant morning breath

your pancakes and eggs please! I'll cry if I keep reminding me. Inhale.

Your room

the last meal we shared

the product used in your baby's hair ! Please

I need to breathe

Too many suffocating memories of you and me.

Grief Over Me

All at one time

I'm suddenly hyper aware of how you feel about me. I think it's the tree.

It makes those obligatory smiles even sadder and slower, Like you're enamoured to your grief instead of me.

And you are.

You're enamored to your grief, Not me.

I think that's why you can't be reached. Cuz I'm trying and I'm reaching Begging

Pleading

Just short of bleeding.

But your lack of presence harshly teaches Me

To be Without you.

In my mind I don't wanna believe that you read this and sighed, More frustrated about wasted time,

And how once again it proves according to you that you need to love better. But then right you turn back into your grief,

Instead of clinging to me. Get the fuck over yourself!

So up Grief's ass you cannot see blessings Or simple things like tea,

Or that I love you so damn much your grief is hurting me. Your grief is hurting me.

And you don't have time for both… It's grief over me.

I'm Sorry to You

People aren't a simple cure for your loneliness kid. Breaking bread with broken people,

Everyday is the same in that regard. Broken people, breaking people.

Isn't that what they did to Jesus?

Broke him because they could not see His love?

I broke a lot of people because I could not see their love.

I'm pretty sure I break Christ's heart every day because I cannot simply be in His love. Who the hell do I think I am?

When did men become my discount Jesus? Why when He show me love I keep refusing it? Brokenness, a drug I been using it.

Addictive to the ego and identity.

Addictive for the broken dreamer writing songs off key. Addictive to me because I don't know my identity.

But I know I've been broken, And distracted.

The devil's favorite tool.

My sins are not redacted but fused with my poet's soul. This thing has holes.

I lament,

Because I want Him to hear me. Feel me.

I need you to heal my brokenness before my soul is gone too. Because It should be a beautiful act,

Breaking bread with broken people, But everyone is yelling louder than me.

Disgusted at my audacity to be broken and silent. More bread for them to eat.

More nights I'm losing sleep, Up lamenting.

While slumber slinks them to their temporary relief. They're the walking dead.

And the thing about brokenness is, Most times you swear you're fine.

I am yours, you are mine. Putting together a broken puzzle. Barefoot, on the floor,

Feeding pieces to each other, fingers to mouth like children do. Only for broken-
ness to have us sin again.

I mean survive again.

My brokenness,

I'm dying now.

I have poisoned the bread somehow. You're dying.

I killed something inside that smiled. My brokenness.

I didn't know. I was a child. I am sorry.

When did men become my discount Jesus? Give me hope in this mess I've made,

Of you.

Of me.

And all the brokenness I've managed to see

And take selfishly finger to mouth like children do. In my brokenness,

I am sorry to me.

I am sorry to you.

Like a Child, I Miss You

Today I could throw a tantrum without you.

Because it is something my heart and mind cannot comprehend. "Without you."

And no matter how many times I try to explain to myself why you are gone, It does not make sense to me.

And the child in me wants to cry. And the romantic in me wants to cry.

And the self-aware adult in me will sob softly wearing a stale mask that I know isn't working too well.

It'd been left out in the open, exposed to every drop of water in the wind. I soaked them in hoping it to be you.

I dried out again realizing they weren't. I could crumple that mask,

But it keeps my face together.

You took my madness and the moon with you. So I really want to throw this tantrum,

I'll throw all the "I miss yous" into the sea. Hoping they'll be tossed, turned, cleaned. Naturally baptized and returned to me.

I'll throw a tantrum on the beach.

Sand in my hair and I wouldn't care as long as I caught it off the wind. An "I miss you too"

Faint and enough to calm my tantrum and the high tide in my eyes, And tamper the sighs so I don't go blowing myself out to sea again. Throwing a tantrum.

Scanning the horizon,

Hanging on word from the wind.

Waiting for the waves to crash into my heart saying that I miss you too. Because I miss you

My stale mask, it crumbles, I miss you. My salted skin, I stumble, I miss you.

I am sorry, like a child, I miss you.

Sleeping Darling

Here is the thing about the sleeping darling, Even as you gush she still sleeps.

You clear sweated curls from her forehead and cheek, And in her grief she sleeps.

Cold tea.

Stale toast.

Sleeping when you need her the most. She is the sleepiest girl in the world.

Unable to break out of her own fever dreams. Eyes crusted over,

Disappointment lined seams.

Nevermind cold compresses when she screams. Nevermind the slight smile in low eyes Morning glory

Breathe.

That is what she does as she sleeps Breathe.

That is all she can handle Breathe.

Rules For When I'm Lonely

1. Don't cut your hair.

2. Don't grasp at straws, leave them boys lonelier than you alone.

3. Silence your phone. Because even though you're alone and hate it, it is an earned feeling.

4. Gasp and whisper apologies to the ceiling.

5. Play the saddest songs, take the deepest sighs all in time to the funeral march for your expectations. Step together. Step together.

6. Move forward at least a lil pinkie toe just so your promise to your mama rings true. "No mama, I won't leave you."

7. Continue to let the water hit your back in the shower as you finish writing this poem. The water is starting to run cold.

8. Take off the scarf you've worn the last 5 days and let your hair breathe, detangle that shit! You've got good hair but damn if it won't dred if you do not work through that shit! Work through your shit!

9. Continue to take up the entire bed when you sleep.

10. Pray the Lord your soul to keep.

The world gets in the way...

Hot Tamale

Hot Tamale,
Like I wasn't folded with care. To keep all the good stuff in. Never mind,
To mama hands. Hot Tamale, eaten every day, somewhere.
But that is how I like it. Husk rushed back Steaming.
And you, smiling hungrily. Unable to wait.
You can't taste the holidays, Or mama's hands,
Or grandma's.
Hot Tamale.
Spicy or sweet to go with you, Or you.
Or you.

Something Borrowed, Something Pink

Something borrowed, Something pink,

Someone stole my innocence I think. Someone stole it.

I'm not really sure cuz I was smiling when it happened.

It took 10 years to see how it hurts when stemmed were snapped off of me. Bud-
ding flower,

Sitting in a tree.

But those flowers grew back, my natural love for pink.

But then with a sick mind, I think

I think

I think I gave my innocence away. Pink goes nice with the color black. That's what
he said but the evening,

The evening it got all jumbled in my head. And I think,

Cheers drink. But I think, Slow blinks.

But I think I gave my innocence away. A natural love for pink,

But he didn't even stay.

Just slurred something about my sloppiness. And i was,

And I stumbled in my door. The pink flowers,

They didn't grow anymore. Because I think,

I think

I think my innocence was killed.

Powerful Magics That Distract You From Yourself

Powerful Magics that distract you from yourself: sex and grief. Symptoms: lack of
sleep,

Shortness of breath.

For me they coincide no less than 85% of the time. I'm not mine.

Causes: overpopulation.

Eternal damnation.

Emotional constipation. I can't feel anything, But sex and grief.

And I'm beautiful so they'll keep coming for me. And I'm ugly so they'll keep com-
ing for me too. Sex and grief til I'm black and blue.

Powerful Magics that distract you from yourself: sex and grief. They're an addic-
tion.

Please, don't tell me that they aren't because in too high a dose of each you'll be
giving away all the things you really need.

Like your worth.

And both things can be done on autopilot. Routine.

We all know what it means:

Dinner, shower, bed.

Open thighs between bedsheets of grief. Try to fall asleep.

Then grief autopilots a similar routine. Dinner, shower, bed.

Open thighs between bed sheets.

Even sad, addicted to a need for intimacy.

Powerful Magics that distract you from yourself: sex and grief. Like accumulation
of wealth it turns into greed.

Like the kind you couldn't possibly spend in a lifetime. I've already told you,

I'm not mine.

I'm yours.

And all of you,

All of you have used me up in this lifetime. And and it hurts.

And I'm not magic.

And it hurts,

When you zone back in from being distracted from yourself.

The Power Dynamics of Panties

I try not to go out of the house in sweatpants. Look nice for a change.

Be nice for a change.

My body aches for intimacy.

But the right kind of touch I can't imagine.

And I'm lying in bed as I write this, unable to turn my face toward the heavens.
Ashamed.

Heavy with hefty fines for growing up too soon. Look nice for a change.

Be nice for a change.

I need change.

I can wash my face.

I can wash my underwear.

I alone cannot wash these sins away. I have been replaced.

By the girl that lives under him. Temporary address.

This is madness.

Because people demanded squatters rights on my person, Under my skin,

In my psyche,

I'll never be rid of them.

I'll never be rid of them.

Do you know how hard it is to get rid of squatters When eyes water at every
"hello pretty lady"?

I never know what to say to me,

To ease anxieties about the opposite sex. The power dynamics of panties,

Too many hands on me.

I have been replaced,

By the girl that lives under him.

Wearing Sunday panties on a Friday to try and feel church. Washing them in the sink,

Washing down my worth, Trying to look nice for a change.

33

A Bad Idea

A morning lament:

This is a very bad idea.

What have I done?

This time to break my own heart. I dream of love,

To live more death.

My big mouth,

Big heart

Naive ways have brought me back here.

Where there are whispers that this is a bad idea. That this is a bad idea.

The beauty marks on me don't mean shit. Unqualified to wear them at best.

Vain because I wear them the least,

Permanently on my skin and I seem to wear them the least. My own beauty marks.

Did you catch that?

I have broken my own heart with impatience. A fool,

I have broken my own heart and can't take it. What tools,

Can I use to save me?

My hands full of issues and tissues.

I don't remember the last time I prayed. That is a bad idea.

This is a bad idea.

Some.

One.

Save.

Until

A longing I'll never be rid of, That's what you are.

I have no picture aside from the one in my dreams, Compelling me to sleep.

I need to be with you.

I'm tired, Father.

I've known longing ever since I was a child.

I wonder sometimes if that is where my longing for you started And just grew.

And spun out of control like my emotions, And all my choices,

Until I met you.

The brief moment I met you. Brief and powerful.

And I lost you.

And I lost me.

And the longing, it grew you see… Until…

Until.

Parallel Universe Me

Parallel universe me, that bitch has my life.

I can feel the ripples of happiness from my choices from here. I haven't seen her since those life changing choices,

Cuz she went that way and I went this way,

but I promise you she is being happy and loud on purpose. She's folding laundry humming.

And actually cooking dinner,

drumming manicured fingernails on kitchen islands And not feeling alone on it.

This me doesn't cook. That one bites her tongue, And is getting married,

Doesn't find submission scary,

And stopped being weary of every good thing come her way. She sighs with knowledge on how to save me,

And has her hands, comforting my baby... My hands feel empty this season.

There's a reason.

This parallel universe isn't far enough away. She is smiling, and not alone.

Her version of the man I loved by her side.

My lip quivering

because I feel the ripples of his adoration and forehead kisses And everythingimiss-
es

Radiating from the universe next door. And Since I'm not smiling…

And I'm not.

Am I the shitty parallel universe neighbor here ? I had chosen all fears,

That life changing split.

I'm a shitty neighbor because what you give is what you get.

Cleanse

Do not be mistaken.

These tears are not for you.

I simply needed to wash you off of me.

But then, I see The Answer...

Life In Sheol

I smiled a lot in Sheol.

I said thank you for a bouquet of flowers full of tongues. Skipped down the street with blood soaked jeans I mean, It was a holiday every day it seemed.

The deflated balloons in the corner were my dreams, A parade of things to show me life is not fair.

I was unaware.

Of life in Sheol.

I smiled a lot.

Fed birds my own eyes,

And sighed so much the wind stopped rushing back into my lungs. I needed to sleep.

Got choked up by bedsheets and "debt paid" panties. And my soul stood guard while I blinked twice for relief, Only to wake and see I was deeper in Sheol.

I still smiled a lot.

They were on to me.

I traveled light.

They were into me and I hadn't looked in the mirror so I did not know, you lose yourself in Sheol.

I bet I taste of salt and shame. They ate me just the same.

Into me, my side hollow.

Ears swallowed all the latest death about me, It rot my teeth.

They had my smile in Sheol.

I watched them sit pretty over my body buffet, They had my smile in Sheol.

I handed them utensils. Thanked them for the bouquet. They had my smile in She-ol.

I was an accomplice.

I could not play life's cards.

I killed my own smile in Sheol.

Crisis of Faith

I'm real deep in a crisis of faith, And that's a real thing to say.

I need to see some righteousness and truth in my adulthood cuz my youth led me to where I am, Here in a crisis of faith.

And that's a real sad thing to say,

Cuz I do love God and light and love and purpose. This world convinced me I'm worthless.

I hear it in my poems, I hear me.

I'm in a crisis of faith.

I'm glad He knows what I want to say,

But I've gotta get over my shame and myself, To live in this holiness,

To get my spiritual wealth. Cuz here I am poor.

And dirty.

And tired.

I am drowning in a crisis of faith.

Or maybe being baptized by my tears.

Cuz I've been crying from things way out of my control. Drowning,

Or being made whole.

I'm growing in my crisis of faith And that's a hard thing to say Because it hurts.

Mustard Seed

I went to church yesterday trying to scare my demons away.

I sat near the back and sang in harmony hymns I didn't know to my mustard seed. They say if you talk to plants they grow.

I need some words for my soul,

And I wrote down all the things I tried not to cry about in church. Because whenever I open my mouth it seems to lessen my worth. Shameful thing.

Mustard seed. I have a need. Grow for me.

A Prayer, A Poem, A Wish

This morning on my way to church a wish came through the window. I held it.

Made a wish.

Made a prayer,

That somehow I'd hear something for me at church that day. Everything about the service was designed to lure me in.

He was speaking poetry.

He had the pastor call on me,

He must have seen the wish on my face. I talked about my crisis of faith.

They laid hands on me and prayed.

I felt my wish on their intentional hands.

I didn't feel me crying until it was too late.

I felt every prayer in the room on me though. They were speaking poetry.

I teared up during a hymn just feeling all the things He knows of me. He knows of me.

He calls me lovely.

I made a wish, He listened.

I made a prayer, He listened. I am committed.

To learn what He knows, To rest in His palm.

I felt my whole soul cry through the hymn. The service.

The message.

The prayer.

The poem..

The wish.

Silent In Sheol

I was not smiling.

I was not breathing.

I was just feeling that he was feeding, all that time in Sheol. And I can fit onto a
plate, cut up for consumption.

Palatable, Needing pepper,

Lazy on the tongue.

That's why I don't get forever kisses, Just the secret ones.

That's how I know my love is missing, I thought I had him once.

We always hungry in Sheol. Fork after fork

Him spider me fly.

Bite after bite,

I wanted to die.

I wanted to die.

Set my wings the way of the purposeless. Proud I could be home on the street.

In the mouth.

Between the teeth.

Not thinking it would be okay if I stepped on tongues from my bouquet. Even if it
made me cry.

Especially because it made me cry. I wanted to die.

I wanted to die.

Let them be silent in Sheol.

They didn't know my name in the first place. Only that I had Many Womens' face.

And Every Man's hands.

And every heartache.

Did every sinful dance.

No, they didn't know my name. They called me what they wanted. Let them be
silent in Sheol.

And surprised I am not dead. Daises blooming from my head.

Watered by His tears as I am carried away like a babe. I could not stay.

Let them be silent in Sheol. Because they didn't know.

I would not stay dead forever.

Sad Girl Spring

Sad girl spring don't mean a thing when your soul is on the line. We out here fighting for my eternal light.

My life:

I swing and miss.

So I'm weak,

But I'm strong too.

Just because I now know whom to look to. Sad girl spring don't mean a thing.

There are still flowers in my hair, And dirt on my feet.

I, humble, feel the heat from my blush at this intimacy. I'm getting to know you.

I'm getting to know me.

Sad girl spring don't mean a thing, When thinking about eternity.

With you,

In the presence of God.

It is true,

I'll think about you forever. I'll dream about you forever, We will live forever,

Like art and God's love.

Like the flowers that you gave me to run through, You gave my heart a home to come to.

Sad girl spring don't mean a thing When your soul knows where to run to.

His Favorite Kind

I prayed myself to sleep two nights in a row, Does that make me a real Christian
now?

Hands full of issues and tissues, Now folded they shrink somehow.

But even bunched up you still take em and dab Your eyes in between strained in-
hales.

Don't forget to breathe.

Don't forget to drink more water love, you weepin for many. Don't forget that in
His eyes you're more than what you see. I prayed myself to sleep.

I prayed for more than peace. My tissues turned to tatters

And my breath matched my heart beat. Air

Water and

Faith all for my mustard seed. I have more than a need.

Now I ache

And that makes me a real Christian. One who knows she cannot see.

Really I should have known better, But being blind,

and bitter.

Rejected, then selected for His peace. That makes it all the better

When my tissues and issues stay tattered on the floor,

And He picks me up and says

"My child, you are so much more."

He'd been screaming that my whole life I bet.

And I told Him I believed I was probably his most stubborn child. Stubborn and
blind

His favorite kind.

Goodbye to Sheol

My life framed by my father wanting himself more, I am weeping at the gates of Sheol,

Lovely and ugly with desire. Am I a tool of the devil?

I've already been a fool of the devil.

Feeling everything, and licking the bars salty from age and tears for sustenance. I'm aching because I know you desire me.

You desire me, Bound by lies Shame Harmless fun

Non traditional violence And blame.

Cursed with desire just the same. I am weeping at the gates of Sheol

Because when you don't know you don't know any better you end up desiring the same. I didn't know my name.

I didn't know my name.

There was power there and I gave it up just the same.

The glamor on Sheol is gone so I'm just weeping for my name. I am crying at this trick.

The devil loves this game.

A girl outside the gates of Sheol, grieving , aching for her own name. God's grace just the same.

He has a list of names.

May he walk with me and give me three, a soul tired babe? Do not panic.

You are standing at the gates of Sheol.

You have your heart and hands let go now of the bars of the gates of Sheol. He calls sings breathes blesses your new name.

Look up.

And walk.

Goodbye to the gates of Sheol.

And I get tears and laughs and art in my eyes...

Say Cheese

In my mind,

I'm no longer surprised

I wake up and feel vivid disappointment to still be here

A morning lament:

I was cursed to feel things deeply

So even the tiniest thing

Can add another crack

To the 30 year old dam

That's me.

Making me unsavory to the eyes of passers by

They give a wide berth to not get wet

Complain to The State that I am an eye sore

Black

And cracked

Leaking water

Exhausted .

Unaware in their ignorance

That if I happen to break

I would devour their town whole.

It does not matter that tourist take my photo,

It is just to marvel in the comfort of their home at my black grief

Of course they don't see it that way…

Just say

Wow, she is still holding up.

That's amazing.

Say cheese.

A novelty, black grief.

And you can't say it isn't because they literally used to make our men fight each other for amusement

And in the same fucking breath mock our women for crying about it.

I don't wanna hear it.

We do not get listened to, only heard.

Black grief ,

Nothing but a word.

And art…

All this art I'm doing lately...

All the moss, and vines and the one tiny flower in a crack on the 30 year old dam that is me…

That is to keep me from dying.

But I'm glad you liked it on Instagram.

I'm glad you sent it to your friends

And said "yo...that girl be writin'

Oh my gosh I'm so in my feels"

Never even paying attention to

I wonder how she feels?

I feel

I feel like a 30 year old dam.

That's Black

And cracked

Leaking water.

And exhausted.

I lament.

Say cheese.

I Was An Angry Black Woman, and All I Got Was This Lousy T-Shirt

God promised no weapon formed against me shall prosper, but what about my own sensitivity? That shit will be the death of me,

For being too nice and thinking twice before I dismiss a person from my life. Cuz if I express any injustice I'm a bitch.

Like take the color brown, add some grief and it's dangerous. War on skin and on mind waging us.

I can't afford that shit.

My tears don't buy a thing.

When grief turns into anger because of melanin, They tell you don't tell anyone,

And it starts to live on your face.

Then people ask why you so mad all the time but don't really listen.

Then ask why you so sad all the time but be too busy licking their own wounds, They miss it.

My black skin told me I was mad before I even knew I was. I thought I was still smiling.

Cuz people mistake my passion and fire for aggression like: "Oh my gosh girl, calm down, it is not that serious."

Bitch dont you know I am sensitive? Like summer rain?

And clay being fired?

My emotions, barbed wire. Simple but still tricky to get over. Raging a war in my fort,

My head, my heart, my soul.

Cuz mine can't spill out like yours,

It would flood the fuckin world whole.

And your concern is why I don't smile more? You'd be mad too,

If you were an angry black woman and all you got was this lousy t-shirt.

Passiveness

Passive friends got me bullied. Passive friends got me assaulted. Passive friends my future altered. Passive me.

Passive me sewed her mouth shut. Passive me felt raw cuts of

Passive you, spitting your own truth at passive me. Passively.

Of course.

I hate that shit !!

And if I hear,"I didn't want to upset you"

Or "I thought you were upset with me" meekly one more time. I think I'd retire being a pacifist.

Get active sis !

Current me actively angry at past passive me for passing up love. Current me actively angry at past passive me for not knowing her worth.

Current me actively angry at current passive you for reminding me of past passive him and his inaction.

Why were we such cowards? Passiveness.

Makes me think I was never really wanted,

That everyone will lack the ability to handle me handling me. And it pisses me off you keep trying !

And it pisses me off I keep letting you !

And you're such a coward you won't even bring it up… And you're such a coward that when you show up, Your hands and heart will be empty.

Empty.

Despite you passively, Despite you passing me, I still had hope.

That won't slip past me again.

The Wrong Definition

I've always had a problem with submission. I answer first,

Then hardly listen.

Rush past bits of me, for you.

Yeaaaaahhh, I've always had a problem with submission. I hardly recognize myself lately,

Heart racing as you taste me

And how does that submission taste ? Better than wasted sugar on counter tops? Coffee creamer?

Lollipops ?

I promise I am more sweet than these if you can get me to submit. So how do you do it?

Well I've always had a problem with submission, So I wont say:

Start at my neck.

Or trace a finger down my spine. Or just listen.

Or keep count with the moon phases. Or growl low dirty phrases in my ear. I'd purr,

But not submit.

Yeah, I've always had a problem with submission I think it's because I've never been loved.

Not enough to listen,

Or not shrink in confusion at your man authority, That has me folded at the waist and no not in a bow, But a laugh that pains my side so much

I need to bend.

I need to bend.

Because I've always had a problem with submission I cannot be submissive because I've never been ready to conform to the authority or will of others.

I don't trust.

It used to make me cry I could not be more submissive, Then I thought maybe I had the wrong definition.

A submissive.

Like, balling my eyes out making sure the place looks spectacular sir. Like, I'm sorry I'll be less emotional, less reactive sir.

Like yes sir.

No sir.

How can I submit sir,

When it is hurting what I know???

Yeaaaaah I've always had a problem with submission. We have yet to truly be introduced.

I not courted.

I don't listen.

But while I remain as so, I will laugh

And laugh, a bended laugh at the ones who dare to try. Yeaaaaaah I've always had a problem with submission.

Tired Girl

From the outside looking in

The trained eye would see a tantrum Of someone tired from carrying Crying from carrying

Way too many Not-For-You Things

But too damn stubborn to put Them down And now you're paralyzed

Stuck little girl.

Barbie and bubblegum in ya pockabook And a book on How-to-Survive The World. Hi, I'm Tired Girl.

My brain rewired girl,

Cuz I been depressed so many times, My brain has to be on fire girl.

So who's gonna save my world? Who's gonna save my world?

I concede, I rebelled it's ways, And I didnt know why.

And now to my detriment I have nearly spent All of my life, unable to live in it comfortably. I don't know how to be here.

No wonder I'm Tired Girl. No wonder I'm Trying Girl. I'm barely surviving, Damn.

Don't know how to cook, Or seriously love a man.

Can't find my fucking niche, I feel so damn incomplete,

I should slap The Mouse himself, And damn near every movie he made, For telling me I'd be special

But not for telling me I'd be so fucking tired girl. I'm so Tired Girl.

You would think I'd build some stamina to keep up with this world.

I am a fast ass girl.

A Hot Tamale,

I know you've heard.

So said the boxes my hips and tits check that say "African American Girl". 'Oh my gosh!

I love your curls!

Did you buy them?

Are they yours?

They couldn't possibly hide secrets on how to heal your generational curse. You look so tired girl!

3, 4 jobs wired girl!

We want you distracted and contracted to your stereotypes, You owe us your life,

And yeah yeah we know you're tired girl!' I am Tired Girl.

Unable to live comfortably in my skin, And no one cares

Because, they all tired girl. Like you.

insert nude

In casual conversation:

I told him I was obsessed with taking nude shots. He told me I was vain.

I ask him what he knew of stretch marks And tear stains

And scars from your youth because you wouldn't leave that shit alone And bitten down fingernails

And funky feet from old shoes

And all the parts that every one insists to pick and chose. I proclaim,

Naw, I'm not vain,

I just love my damn self.

Busy Being Black

I'm sorry.

I don't have any more poems. I was busy being Black.

And you would think I could manage both, Are they not one in the same ?

Living life and not sure how to explain how you feel? So you write it.

Anger Worry Depression

Burning questions like:

"Where I come from?"

And

"Why don't my hair look like that too?" I'm sorry.

I have no time.

I can't explain my born-with-attitude face And hips

As they rush off busy busy busy My face busy busy

Holding in my rolling eyes, And dart like tongue

And historic hums And all my rights

And the safe path at night so my hips don't go telling someone something
that ain't for them.

I. Am. Busy.

I'm sorry.

I don't have anymore poems.

I was busy fighting in a slave rebellion Hell bent on taking back freedom

That was lost in the arrogance,

The idea that it is still someone's to take. Excuse my black.

Excuse my quake

As I scream "I am not yo nigga gal"

For every ancestor still at unrest.

Being Black I used to think that God made a mistake,

Cuz no one with this much hardship should be doomed to be tar ugly, And nappy headed,

Big nosed, Name: Dreaded,

Because I am the least desired demographic. How tragic.

I am tired.

I am busy.

Cuz being black you gotta be twice as good to go half as far, And I feel like I've already traveled a lifetime.

Cried a lifetime

Lived a lifetime of poetry, Of half histories,

Of not knowing me

Of continued fight for you and me Because we are Black

And instead of warranting praise it warrants more attack! But we are paying the same taxes,

Waving the same flag.

Pretty Ms. Becky is wearing the same damn thing,

But its my black ass getting dragged across the "still not good enough"coals. So I am sorry.

I don't have anymore poems. I was busy being Black.

Just Sit and Write

I have been looking for myself lately. I was wearing so my faces.

Some sad.

Some mad.

Some that looked as if they did not know love.

Silly me thinking childhood would stain my face forever, I must stop crying.

And look at me as new. That is the only way to see. Stop crying child,

That is the only way to see. Look.

The grateful in the skies and the trees. Look.

The grateful in the love you have received, As you do nothing but breathe.

You are new.

I do a lil alchemy...

A Collection of Short Stories

The Traveler in Black America

I was extremely tickled about riding city transit. I looked out the big windows, giggled to myself when someone tugged the line to stop and though a woman of twenty-two my feet didn't touch the floor, so I swung them back and forth, a way to release my excitement.

I saw a lady, a character more like it. She had a very short ponytail, the ends of her hair and her "kitchen" was burned by perm. Her big southern lips, much like a catfishes', had matriculated spit as she chatted with Da Man sitting diagonally from her. She wore a white tee with a stressed neck and lint ball lined armpits. It seemed to be her own personal style to wear one gold hoop earring and one silver. Her thong sandals had her foot permanently imprinted in them and her feet were scrapped white. Her jean shorts worn, worn from bus travel, worn from her striped thighs. Worn. Tired.

"Oh shit shit shit shit!" Down went her Arizona Southern Style Sweet Tea. Da Man sitting diagonally had picked up her tea, but not before she had a chance to drop her bottle of white and green pills on the bus seat. They seemed more important to her than tea.

Da Man's arrogance: "You didn't say thank you, I picked up your tea". "Ooooh thank you baby baby baby", she slurred.

Her big brown purse had the zipper chewed on a bit, the leather broken away in parts and a safety pin keeping the strap from giving up entirely. She pulled out loose bills. She counted her money. She counted her money again. She nodded. She nodded again. She slept. When was the last time she slept?

"You see her?" said Da Man to Me and Frequent Rider, "What a mess. She fell asleep." "She drops that money…Imma take it".

My reply: "Don't do that, that's not right."

"No! What's not right is getting on the bus THAT HIGH!!" and he pointed right in her face, she didn't even flinch. I hoped the money hung onto her fingers tighter than she was hanging onto it. "Ma'am? Ma'am? Wake up.", I pleaded.

Da Man is tired: "No! Don't wake her! Ima take that money!" "Ma'am? Ma'am?" I cared.

Bung! Snyder Street. That was his stop. The money dropped. He scooped up most of it and sauntered off the bus smooth. I recalled her saying a few stops earlier, "Snyder. Is this Snyder?…No? okay okay okay, cuz thas my stop, my stop." Da Man was generous enough to not take all of her money so I picked up the rest and put it in the chewed purse. That was her stop too. Snyder Street, the same stop. Damn.

The Frequent Riders attempted to ease my obvious distress, "Don't be upset, I mean Da Man was right, she shouldn't of come on the bus high. Stuff like this happens all the time…" He continued to tell a similar tale he had witnessed months ago. "I mean I really don't think it's any of my business", He continued. Then he shrugged, "Oh well. I wonder if she'll even realize anything is missing, she is so high."

My face now blurred with every other tired one on the bus.

Raazen only wore white and whenever I asked her why she insisted that every other color hurt her. "Whites pure, clean n das exactly what I need", she'd say. On the other hand she loved seeing me in colors. My favorite was when she would put rainbow beads on the ends of my braids and maybe once a year I would see her wear an orange hair wrap. I didn't understand but, she said color meant something different for me.

We stayed in a small two bedroom apartment with one of her "associates". Ugly salmon colored walls, crummy tile in the bathroom, funky carpet that smelled like dirty underwear and "Temptress", Raazens favorite perfume. There was no phone, a mattress with no box spring or bed frame and a worn out couch that I slept on in the living room. Only one of the eyes on the stove worked and we each had our own spoon, fork, bowl and plate. Mine was pink and had princess Jasmine and Rajah on it.

I loved living with my sister and as little sister, my adoration knew no end. We always played dress up and pretend. We would pretend we lived in Elysian Fields, the wealthy neighborhood across the street. Big beautiful brick houses, with a tennis court, and swimming pool, and during the holidays they would always string lights in the manicured bushes and place a big wreath with a red bow on all the lamp posts. Walking by you see family vans, bikes in the yard, pets. Life.

Back in our world, we danced in the mirror to N' Sync and giggled like we both were six years old. When Raazen danced it's like she tuned out the rest of the world. She swayed her hips, her hands rubbing different parts of her body. I tried dancing like her once and she slapped me, hard. "Don't you eva, EVA le me see you dancin like dat again," she yelled. This confused me, made me angry so I yelled back, "Why?! I only wanna be like you!".

"DAMMIT!!," now she was crying too. She scooped me up and we melted into the mattress. "No, no baby you don't wanna be anythin like me," she whispered. "I want you have self-respect. Love yaself Tay.

Love yaself, and never stop bein you." I never forgot that day. It made me curious. What was so wrong with her that she didn't want me to be like her?

One day when I was nine Raazen slept longer than usual, and I was bored. Into her room i sleath crawled. Her room was a mess. I started to line up all her perfume bottles first, then hung her purse from the doorknob, then put all her jewelry back in its box. She snored heavily, so I tried not to snicker as I snoop cleaned. Usually she doesn't allow me in her room after she works the night shift when she's sleeping, I quickly learned why.

She had bras, panties, feathers everywhere. What baffled me was that they were all kinds of colors. Red, yellow, green, blue, purple, pink, black. On the floor next to her were big wads of cash. I took in all the colors around her. Drowning her, strangling her, punishing her. It was like someone punched me in the throat. I couldn't breathe, I couldn't think about anything else but the fact that she could be hurt. In a panicked haze I began to snatch up the bras and panties and throw them into the hall. Raazen sprang up.

"Baby…what you doin in my room?" she said quietly.

I noticed her body. Boney, different colors on her skin. Red, yellow, green, blue, purple, pink, black. "These colors. I'm right, you're hurt! Where's your white!?"

I didn't even wait for the answer; I dashed out the door into the January air to find her help. Raazen wasn't far behind me, yelling at me to stop running so she could explain, so we could talk. I was running so hard two of my braids lost their beads and decorated the crosswalk.

Skeeeert smash! A pearl Lincoln Town car had sent Raazen flying through the air. Through the blur I could see a more vivid display of red, yellow, green, blue, purple, pink, black veil her skin.

All the people in the beginning of Elysian Fields came out of their houses. "Nosy pricks" as Raazen would say. She'd been hurting. She'd been hurting and hid it well. I watched them as they placed her into a body bag and drive her away, no sirens. Last thing I remember was the cold, feeling so damn cold.

Taking it Back

You so nice I had to blush twice:

After remembering and grieving the parts of my garden that bore weeds, I smiled and laughed at my budding daisy seed.

An authentic throwback Alyshia moment.

I was mad crushing on a guy I used to work with and he was crushing too. It was baaaaaaaaaaaad and everyone could see it. Though nothing came of it, it is my favorite version of me counter a man. We had laughs and pleasant conversation at work. He was helpful, and silly and of course handsome. Protective and kind. I never felt pressured for anything more, never felt disrespected, I was the woman, the very young woman. Eventually he moved away, the day I found out he was leaving I couldn't even look at him at work without...laughing. I had never in my life had such a reaction. Nervous laughter lol Nervous. Cute. Cute little budding daisy laughter.

I am too romantic to not plant more daisies on me, Or to keep growing towards the sky.

Deeply rooted in good soil, I root deep so no one will take me. No fences because the world needs reminding of innocent love. Fellow romantics smiling at the daisies.

Even when it rains, a romantic will always plant more seeds. Tend them with his kind words and kind heart.

An innocent love.

Daisies with ease.

Change of Heart

"You're going to fall in love with me." Huh? Confidence or arrogance, could you repeat that please?

"You are going to fall in love with me." "No, I promise I'm not."

Who the hell did this guy think he is??? He then explained how every girl he's been kind to, opens himself up to, falls madly in love with him and he ends up not feeling the same.

Yawwwwwwn. I had the same story, and I too had instructed, damn near warned people : do not fall in love with me. But me? Fall in love with a slightly Cooler Carlton Banks ? Falso.

I got even more of a chuckle when his little sister said the same thing weeks later. "You're gonna fall in love with my brother you know, every girl does", she said really fast. "Oh, I'll be fine. I think it is your brother who has to worry about me. "

She shook her head slowly, and raised her eyebrows. She had a face that said I didn't know what I was up against. What, did Cooler Carlton have a secret weapon? Was he successful, a man with vision, educated, thoughtful, a great provider and listener, could code switch with ease and be bomb in the bedroom ?? My very preoccupied heart, and mind doubted it. I decided his comment was arrogant, not confident, and spent the next few months proving him wrong. I did not fall in love. Not with him or any other suitors who caught my attention but briefly. After a while I ended up with someone else entirely. That sure showed him. Hmph.

I've come to believe my stubbornness has kept me from some of the sweetest, and gentlest of men.

Recoiling from real love or connection because the hurt in me made everything sound like a challenge. Including loving me. Especially loving me. But he did not. "I think it is you who should be careful.", I had said. But he never saw it as a challenge, and he knew he would be careful.

"You're gonna fall in love with me you know ", Hmmm. There was the sentence again, popping in my mind just about 2 years later. Cool Carlton had stopped his pursuit long ago when he correctly labeled me as a Hurt Helen. A Hurt Helen that needed a bunch of time to herself to sort her shit. Smart man. But now I found him annoying for it, like how dare he. Proclaim I'm going to fall in love then do NOTHING to make me fall in love? And call me correctly a Hurt Helen?! The-the tease! The child ! And for that matter, why the HELL would he lump me with every other silly little girl who darkened his DMs with heart emojis and proclamations of love? ahahaha yeah, it annoyed me.

Then, not that long ago I saw he did and he was. He did all the things for the long game to make me fall in love with him:

He respected himself enough to leave me alone when I was toxic. Still showed love and care from a distance.

Recognized my vulnerability and knew women and me enough to know how easy it is to "fall in love" when vulnerable.

He didn't prey on me.

But I bet he's prayed for me and ya know, he had never treated me as what I was. A Hurt Helen. I bet he'd been in love with me this entire time and i just didn't know. I bet there was something prophetic in his "you're gonna fall in love with me you know." There is so much more to that

sentence now. What I saw as arrogance was him speaking time. He was speaking healing, growth and future to me. He was calling his wife. He was calling me his wife.

I want you

I think he was the only one that meant it in the way that it was supposed to mean.
A simple phrase whispered and thought by many, and here it was, in my ear, off
the lips of a 19 year old boy. Yet, I think he was the only one that meant it in the
way that it should mean. It could be argued that neither of us knew what it meant,
really, especially with us feeling so compelled to sneak to the dim basement of my
father's house to have this conversation. We were babies. But we did know, he did,
he said it, and I believed him. The summer was always hot in Georgia, so we
smelled like outside cooled by AC. I was standing close to him, he was leaning
close to me. How does one respond to forever at 19, and he's even 3 months
younger than me. 10 seconds later he was holding my waist like the good little
country boy he was, and he said I love you in a way that I'm only hearing now, a
decade later. He was silent, like he wanted to get in time with my heart beat first.
Like he had to replay our first time meeting at age 3 and grieve the 7 years we
spent not knowing how the other was doing first. Our lips were a sigh a part and
he didn't move and was silent...like he wanted to say this since age 3, like he want-
ed to love all the pain away from me...like he meant it. Because he did. I felt it.
Something in him changed. "I want you ", he said. He was the only one who said it
and meant it in the way it is supposed to mean. "I want you". It sounded like long-
ing and us giggling in church pews at age 6 again. "I want you " Those kisses tasted
like he wanted to want me forever, even if he had me. Why did I run? I couldn't
take the intimacy. He had showed me his heart and I ran. This 19 year old boy, 3
months younger than me had taught me something important about love.

Accidental Church

I am a women's woman, amen.

3 stories of accidental church I need now and needed then:

1

Ms. B is sweet. She's got those dainty piano hands that I always wished I had. We both have a sun tattoo and she's got her own kind of badass, otherwise I would not feel so compelled to be her friend. We had accidental church while a sermon spilled in the background one Sunday. In all reality the sermon was probably very eloquently stated, not spilled. It was us who spilled, right onto the steps and right into conversations uplifting one another, frustrations and confirmation who thee f we are, as young budding women.

In proper church fashion there were giggles, a few swear words on my part and a double dare. That's proper girl church that is. We related in more ways than I thought. I kept circling back to her words of "we were born to do this". It applied to both her situation and mine though I'm unsure whether she realized it. Both of us on different cusps of womanhood. Both realizing something very honest, we both were tired and needed to come to church. It met us where we were, there on the stairs.

2

"Help me take out my braids?" Is there anything else that says I love you amongst girlfriends? We sit in a circle on the floor.

Cut. Unravel. Open up.

We cut the braid of not quite our hair as short as we can, Another unravels the rest of the braid.

Finally she opens up the hair that was tucked away. Happy to have her scalp breathe.

Accidental church for you and me. Cutting off the old.

Unravelling secrets and sins. Stories, amends.

Opening up to perspective and healing, and happy to be able to breathe. Accidental church with my girls, us 3.

3

4 generations in the kitchen. Umi, Mommy, me and niece.

All the fierce women ancestors are pleased. What a way to start the new year.

Umi, mommy, me and niece. All smiles. All peace.

Me and umi fantasized about the East.

Mommy and I had our own Prince concert, spoons our mic. And me and niece did as we pleased,

which consisted of harassing everyone with the same mischievous girl grin and cackle at our job well done.

Umi, mommy, me and niece.

Yanna Jae

Yanna Jae wears her hair this and thataway Yanna Jae wears an attitude

At least that's what her face say…

Yanna Jae sat across from me in 7th grade English, and because of the alphabet, next to me in homeroom, Social Studies, Spanish…mainly anytime the teacher felt the need to adhere to the alphabet, there we were, from middle school to high school. I can still hear her laugh to this day, though I haven't seen her in at least a decade. She laughed at our English teacher, the weird kid a few tables over, at her friends who were waaaaaaaay over there sharing the inside joke of the week and she laughed at me, and I never really cared.

I saw her. She was another black girl ally in our predominantly white school and my first example of black girl magic. I had the privilege to witness her change, grow, both real close but far away because I can't say we were ever really friends, but here's what I saw:

She was scrappy, but whenever I heard she got into a fight, I wondered who provoked her. She did have a temper. But just:

Don't embarrass her.

Don't come at her disrespectful. Don't be all in her space.

She would cry, and her leg would be shaking and just breathing into her clenched fists. Holding her anger back and self together at the same time. The plight of the black woman it seems.

She was sensitive. There were days she would come into class quiet, more quiet than normal, I never knew her home life but I recognized the silence. I caught tears a few years later as break up whispers did their high school thing. I caught her crying with joy when so inspired. She would cover her smile with her hand, even after she got her braces off.

She was smart, made good grades. Quick to point out an injustice to her person, it left her sparing with teachers and students at times. Maybe the word is witty? I saw it as a much needed defense, seeing as how the teachers ended up apologizing, a lot. And the students, they just ended up sorry they tried. I found it poetic. She would not be guilted into anything, and was not playing around.

She was fashionable. I remember at a point in high school I was in my own mirror wishing I could pull off the many looks Yanna J had. She changed her hair, her bags, her whole vibe it seemed every quarter. She could be a Chris Brown back up dancer one day, then Holister cozy the next in a hoodie, then in shades, a hat and belt looking like Auntie Mary J Blidge, then Jordan's, basic tee and tight jeans. And they all seemed like her…

I easily saw the houses in her that I wouldn't see, understand or accept in myself until college. She exemplified the vastness that is the beauty that is the young black woman. I saw her. Even back then my mind was writing poems, stories, narration to my dramatic and confusing teenage years. I recognized that I was witnessing something real intimate, just knowing her, but was not sure of the name of such art. "Living." I admired her unapologetic black girl living.

Yanna Jae wears her hair this and thataway, Yanna Jae wears an attitude

At least that's what her face say… Her beautiful black girl face...

And I am left with just me.

I see you Mocha Mocha.

About the Author

Alyshia Bradley is a 30 year old Artistic Renaissance Woman from Lusby, Maryland. She graduated top of her College at Coppin State University in 2015 with a Bachelor's of Science Degree in Urban Arts. Though a performer in many facets: musician, singer, actress, Alyshia will always see herself as a writer first. Throughout her adolescence, books by Toni Morrison and Maya Angelou turned her thoughts into lyrics, stanzas. Never seeking these women, but by some serendipity, their works found her and changed her for the better. Mesmerized by their warm but powerful tones, relatable stories, and narratives Alyshia learned early on, perspective matters. Also an advocate for The Arts, Alyshia uses her platform to shine light on the importance of art for the sake of humanity, as well as a coping tool for mental health issues, especially within the African American community. "Being human art has given me a great vulnerability and a great responsibility to tell what it is I am experiencing. I have the greatest purpose in the world! Love people and teach them to turn pain into art. People want to know that they will make it, and that they aren't alone. I want to know that too. It is why write, to make my humanness bearable when it isn't. That pain unites us all and I find that beautiful."